W9-BZA-329

J133.1   c.2
Coh   Cohen, Daniel,
                Young ghosts

                          1399

FEB - - 1995

Mount Laurel Library
Mount Laurel, N.J. 08054
Phone 234-7319

DEMCO

YOUNG GHOSTS

Children have always been fascinated by ghosts. This painting, by the eighteenth-century artist Sir Joshua Reynolds, shows a child impersonating a ghost.

lb 13.99
88525

ILLUSTRATION CREDITS

The Bell Witch of Tennessee by Charles Bailey Bell (A Descendant), 62; The Granger Collection, New York, 98; Harry Price Library, University of London, 42; New York Public Library, 16, 56, 72, 81; Radio Times Hulton Picture Library, *ii*, 46; Marc Seifer, *Journal of Occult Studies, vi*; Society for Psychical Research, 26.

Copyright © 1978, 1994 by Daniel Cohen
All rights reserved
No part of this book may be reproduced in any form
without permission in writing from the Publisher.

Library of Congress Cataloging-in-Publication Data
Cohen, Daniel, date
Young ghosts / Daniel Cohen—2nd ed.
p.   cm.
Includes bibliographical references and index.
ISBN 0-525-65154-3
1. Ghosts—Juvenile literature.   [1. Ghosts.]   I. Title.
BF1461.C669   1994
133.1—dc20   93-45924   CIP   AC

Published in the United States by Cobblehill Books,
an affiliate of Dutton Children's Books,
a division of Penguin Books USA Inc.
375 Hudson Street, New York, New York 10014

Designed by Mina Greenstein
Printed in the United States of America
First Edition   10 9 8 7 6 5 4 3 2 1

YOUNG GHOSTS

REVISED EDITION

Daniel Cohen

Illustrated with
photographs and prints

Mount Laurel Library
100 Walt Whitman Avenue
Mt. Laurel, NJ 08054-9539

COBBLEHILL BOOKS

Dutton   New York

CONTENTS

Introduction   1

1]   Radiant Boys   4
2]   The Avenging Ghost   17
3]   Ghost Hunters' Stories   27
4]   Rosalie   36
5]   Reverend Wesley's Poltergeist   52
6]   The Bell Witch   63
7]   Christmas Ghosts   78
8]   Some American Ghosts   90

Bibliography   103
Index   104

A spirit photograph of ghostly children, from Photographing the Invisible *by James Coates. Photos of this type were popular in the late nineteenth century.*

Introduction

CHILDREN HAVE ALWAYS HAD A SPECIAL relationship to ghosts. No, it is not that children are more likely to believe in ghosts than adults. Plenty of adults believe in ghosts; they are just less willing than children to admit that they do. What this book is concerned with is the enormous amount of ghost lore which involves children. Either the children are ghosts or the children see ghosts, or the presence of a child somehow appears to trigger ghostly events.

Now at this point I confess to being somewhat embarrassed. I have written many books on various aspects of ghost lore. At the beginning of nearly all of them I find myself explaining that all of the stories you are about to read are true, but . . .

Well, if you have read some of my other ghost books, you probably know what I'm going to say already. So you can skip the explanation and get right on to the ghosts. If not, please bear with me for the next few paragraphs. I think it is very helpful if the reader knows the sort of material that he or she is getting into. It is also only fair that the writer level with his readers. And I won't detain you long with explanations and excuses.

As I have said, all the stories you are about to read are true, but . . . What I mean is that at one time or another all of these stories have been represented as being true. None of them is avowedly fiction. It seems pretty obvious that some of the accounts, however, are not true—perhaps none of them are true, or at least not accurate. There may be some explanation other than a ghost for what people reported. But the stories in this book do represent what people, at least some people, have believed, and still believe.

Though the topic is limited to children and ghosts, the range of tales is a broad one. They are not of equal value as evidence for ghosts. Some of the stories, like those of the Radiant Boys, or some of the Christmas ghosts, are based on very slim evidence. On the other hand, the evidence for those stories that came from the files of the Society for Psychical Research is really rather good—as good as it gets for ghosts anyway. These chapters will show you just how people in different places and different times reacted to the notion of ghosts.

I'm not trying to prove or disprove the existence of ghosts in this little book. People have been arguing about that for a long time now. My aim is very simple: It is to present for your entertainment and perhaps your enlightenment some tales of children and ghosts.

These stories are not meant to make you scream in terror or to give you nightmares. But if, after reading this book, you hesitate just a bit longer before entering a darkened room, or wonder what that noise you just heard outside your bedroom door *really* is, then I have accomplished my purpose.

ONE

Radiant Boys

OF ALL THE LEGENDS OF GHOSTLY CHILD-
ren the strangest, and dare I say the most haunting,
is that of the Radiant Boys.

A Radiant Boy is an apparition or a vision of a
young boy surrounded by a glowing flame or light.
The sight of such a figure is greatly feared. It is supposed to mean that the person who sees it will die a
violent death. Other accounts hold that those who see
the figure will experience a period of great power,
which will end in violent death. In either case, the
Radiant Boy is considered a very evil omen.

There is no general agreement as to whether the
Radiant Boys are really ghosts or some other kind of

spirit. Some say they are the ghosts of children murdered by their parents. Others believe that they are
not truly ghosts at all, but some other form of supernatural creature from the spirit world that was never
alive but has merely taken the form of a human child.
In any case, tales of Radiant Boys are fairly common
in Germany and some of the other Northern Euro-
pean countries. Belief in these spirits was probably
brought to England by immigrants from those lands.
In England the belief has flourished.

Unquestionably the most celebrated and sinister
of the English Radiant Boy stories concerns the apparition's appearance to the early nineteenth-century
English statesman, Viscount Castlereagh.

When he was a young man, before he assumed
the title of Viscount, he was known as Captain Robert
Stewart, second son of the Marquis of Londonderry.
He spent a great deal of time in Ireland, where his
father owned large tracts of land. One day, while the
young man was out hunting, he lost his way, just as
a storm broke. Castlereagh was fortunate enough to
find a house nearby. Though he had never been to
the house before, he knocked on the door and asked
for shelter from the rain.

The house was already filled with guests, some of
whom, like Castlereagh, had been caught in the storm.
But the host said that he was sure his butler could
find an extra bed somewhere. The son of a large land-

owner, even the second son, could not be turned away.

After a good dinner and some pleasant conversation with the many guests, Castlereagh was shown to his room. It was quite large and had a fireplace, but there was something strange about the room. However, Castlereagh was far too tired to worry about the oddness of his quarters. He was just happy to be out of the rain. He quickly fell asleep before the blazing fire.

After being asleep for about two hours, Castlereagh was awakened when the light suddenly seemed to flare up. At first he was alarmed because he thought the room was on fire. But when he looked in the fireplace he found that the fire had gone out.

The bright light was coming from the form of an extremely beautiful boy who was standing near the fireplace, and seemed to be gazing intently at him. As Castlereagh watched, the light began to fade until it and the boy's form disappeared entirely.

Castlereagh's first reaction was fear and wonder; but as he thought about what had happened, he became angry. He believed that his host or someone else in the house had gone to great trouble to play a practical joke on him. Throughout his life Castlereagh was known as a suspicious man with absolutely no sense of humor.

The following morning Castlereagh announced his intention to leave at once. His host could tell that the

Lord Castlereagh was awakened by a lovely shining figure of a child by his bed.

young man was extremely angry, and asked him what had happened. Grudgingly, Castlereagh told of his experience, adding that he was sure he had been the victim of a hoax or practical joke. His host seemed inclined to agree but insisted that he had nothing to do with it. The other guests were questioned, but all swore they knew nothing of the glowing figure.

Finally, the host called his butler. He asked the servant where Castlereagh had slept. Rather haltingly the butler admitted that he had put the guest in "the boy's room," because there was no other space available. But he added that he had lit a blazing fire to keep "him" out.

The owner of the house was furious. He reminded the butler of his strict instructions that under no circumstances was anyone ever to be put in "the boy's room."

He then took Castlereagh aside to explain what had happened. He told the young man that the glowing form was the spirit of one of his ancestors. Many years ago the boy, who was only nine or ten at the time, had been murdered by his own mother during a fit of madness. The murder had taken place in the very room in which Castlereagh had spent the night. Since then, from time to time, the boy's blazing spirit had been seen by people who spent the night in the room.

But there was more to tell, and this part of the

story the host related very slowly and reluctantly. The appearance of the flaming phantom was thought to be an evil portent to anyone who saw it. It meant two things. First, the person would have a period of great prosperity and power. But at the height of his power he would die violently.

The news did not greatly trouble Castlereagh. He was extremely brave, and not at all superstitious. He simply did not believe what he had been told. As the second son of the Marquis of Londonderry, he was not destined to be heir. His older brother was in good health. In the normal course of events, he would be neither prosperous or powerful. All he could look forward to was a military career, in which a violent death might be expected.

But within a few years the young captain's prospects took a dramatic turn. His eldest brother was drowned in a boating accident and he became heir apparent, adopting the honorary title of Viscount Castlereagh.

Castlereagh left the army and went into politics. He displayed a talent for politics that no one had previously suspected he possessed. Very rapidly Viscount Castlereagh became one of the most powerful men in England.

But power did not bring him happiness. Castlereagh was widely disliked, even by his political allies. Part of the problem was his cold and hostile manner.

He was a complicated and enigmatic person. By 1822 his contradictory nature, and the great strains of his work, began to break him down. Always a suspicious man, he became violently so. He saw plots everywhere, and today he would be described as paranoid. His mental state became so alarming that he was confined to his country home. His family feared that he would kill himself and all razors and other sharp objects were removed from his room. But on August 12, 1822, Viscount Castlereagh found a small penknife and used it to cut his own throat.

There is another version of the story that was often told by the author Edward Bulwer-Lytton (later Baron Lytton of Knebworth). The family's ancestral home, Knebworth, was said to have been haunted by several ghosts.

Bulwer-Lytton had a lifelong interest in ghosts and other supernatural subjects, and wrote excellent ghost stories. He also regularly entertained, and frightened, his guests at Knebworth with the Castlereagh tale, which he claimed was absolutely true.

According to Bulwer-Lytton, Castlereagh had stayed at Knebworth during his grandfather's time. One morning Castlereagh came down to breakfast looking haggard and pale. He told his host that he had seen a strangely dressed boy with long yellow hair sitting in front of the fire in his room. The boy drew his fingers across his throat three times. A short time later, Castlereagh cut his own throat.

After telling the story, Bulwer-Lytton would then ask his guests if one of them would mind sleeping in "the haunted room." Bulwer-Lytton called the phantom the Yellow Boy. Those who had the courage to accept the challenge usually spent a sleepless night. Even without a ghost the room was spooky. According to one who had seen the room, it "was panelled in dark oak, the furniture funereal. The wardrobe, huge in dimensions, was like an inverted hearse."

An artist who slept in the room was so terrified that he could not bring himself to open the wardrobe for fear of what he might find inside. He just sat up all night with his clothes on, staring at the thing.

Another visitor, the painter E.M. Ward, knew of the wardrobe. He threw open the door and was horrified when a large pot fell out and crashed on the floor. Ward got a second shock when he looked in the mirror and saw, above his own, another face staring at him. It took the terrified Ward a moment to recognize that the second face was that of his host. Bulwer-Lytton had crept into the room and stood silently behind him. The author was famous for his rather peculiar sense of humor.

But perhaps Ward saw or experienced more than he ever told. Later he, too, committed suicide.

Radiant Boys have another, and more direct, connection with the Lytton family. One of Bulwer-

Lytton's eighteenth-century ancestors, Thomas Lytton, was known in his own day as the Bad Lord Lytton. It was a title he earned. He was reported to have seen one of the flaming apparitions shortly before the end of his dissipated life.

The figure of a boy dressed in white appeared beside his bed one evening and announced that he had very little time to live. "How long?" demanded Lytton. "Weeks, months, perhaps a year?"

"You will die within three days," replied the figure.

Lytton was naturally alarmed and depressed by the prediction. He told his servants and friends about it, but tried to maintain a brave front, saying that he had never felt better in his life.

As he went to bed at eleven in the evening of the third day, Lord Lytton was almost beginning to feel cheerful. "If I live over tonight, I shall have jockeyed the ghost, for this is the third day," he told his servant.

The servant left the room briefly. When he returned he found his master was having a choking fit. Lytton had been subject to such fits before, and the servant might have been able to help him. But with the ghost's prediction weighing on his mind, the terrified servant dashed from the room, and Lytton died before the clock struck midnight.

There was another supernatural event connected with Lytton's death. One of his friends, Miles Peter

Andrews, lived nearby. He knew of the ghost's prediction, and had seen that Lytton had been badly
affected by it.

On the night Lytton died, Andrews himself was
not feeling too well and went to bed early. He had
almost dropped off to sleep when the curtains of his
bed were suddenly drawn back and he saw Lord Lytton standing there. Andrews' first thought was that
he was being made the butt of some sort of practical
joke. Lord Lytton had a reputation for elaborate practical jokes.

"You are up to some of your tricks," he told the
figure. "Go to bed, or I'll throw something at you."

The figure looked at him gravely and said, "It's
all over with me, Andrews."

Andrews threw a slipper at the figure, but it glided
silently out of the room. Even after Andrews inspected
the room and found all the doors and windows locked,
he still suspected that it had been a trick. It was only
the next day when he heard of Lord Lytton's death
that Andrews realized that what he had experienced
was not a joke at all. It was several years before he
recovered from the shock of the incident.

THE MOST PERSISTENT Radiant Boy legends
in England have come from a place called Corby
Castle in the county of Cumberland. The "castle"
really looks more like a country manor house, which

is what it is. But the site on which the house standshad been used as a fortification since Roman times. Part of the ruins of a tower built by the Romans are incorporated into the structure of the present house. The room said to be haunted by the Radiant Boy is in the older part of the house, adjoining the Roman tower.

No one is sure when or how the tales of the Radiant Boy of Corby Castle began. But the last reported appearance of the specter took place in September of 1803. The Howard family, who had owned Corby for many years, held a large house party. The house was crowded and the haunted room was given to the Rector of Greystoke and his wife. The Howard family knew of the room's ghostly tradition, but had never taken it seriously.

On the morning after their arrival, the rector and his wife departed in great haste. They refused to give an explanation as to why they were behaving so strangely.

A few days later Howard visited the rector and tried to find out what had happened. The clergyman, who had recovered somewhat from his shock, was able to talk about the night he had spent in the haunted room. He told Howard that in the middle of the night, he was awakened by a bright flame. Like others who have confronted the Radiant Boy, the rector first thought the room was on fire. But then he saw a boy with long golden hair and all clothed in white standing near the bed. The boy was simply staring at him. After a few minutes the figure glided to the wall and disappeared.

The Rector of Greystoke was so terrified by the experience that he had to flee from the house first thing in the morning. He was also embarrassed. Clergymen were not supposed to see ghosts or spirits. He made Howard promise never to speak publicly of the incident.

Howard held his tongue, but the rector didn't. In a few months he was telling the story to anyone who would listen.

This is one ghost story with a happy ending. The Radiant Boy's appearance did not seem to have any ill effects on the Rector of Greystoke. Not only did he fail to die violently, twenty years later he was still going around to house parties telling of his encounter with the Radiant Boy of Corby Castle. But most of the guests had already heard it.

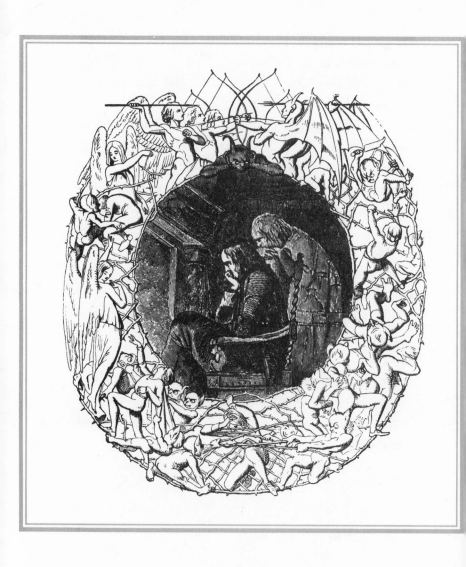

*Many well-known writers have written ghost stories.
This is an illustration from Charles Dickens' story
"The Haunted Man."*

TWO

The Avenging Ghost

THE SPIRIT THAT COMES BACK FROM THE grave to right some wrong is a stock figure of supernatural fiction. But at one time many people believed that such things actually happened, and happened quite often.

Two or three hundred years ago, accounts of such incidents were written up in little books called penny tracts. They were very popular. The title of one pamphlet printed in 1670 speaks for itself: *Strange and Wonderful news from Lincolnshire. Or a Dreadful Account of a Most Inhumane and Bloody Murther, committed upon the Body of one Mr. Carter by the Contrivance of his elder Brother, who had hired three more villains to committ the Horrid Fact, and how it was soon after found out by the Appearance of a Most Dreadful and Terrible Ghost, sent by Almighty Providence for the Discovery.* In the seventeenth century you didn't have to read all the way through a book to find out what was going to happen.

But it wasn't just the penny pamphlets that contained such accounts. They could be found in court records as well. There are numerous cases where guilty persons, who might have otherwise escaped punishment, confessed because they said that their victim's ghost appeared to them. In other cases the ghost appeared to a third party with a denunciation or some clue which led to the conviction of a criminal.

There are many cases in which ghosts are said to have appeared in order to protect their widows and children from dishonest trustees or greedy relatives.

The ghost, therefore, served a very useful role in society. Murderers with guilty consciences, who feared being accused by a ghost, confessed; or they actually began to believe that they had seen one. People who harbored unprovable suspicions were able to speak out if they said they had gotten information from a ghost. Many, many crimes must have been deterred simply from a fear of avenging ghosts. Perhaps it would be a good thing if more people believed in such ghosts today.

One of the most well-documented of the many

avenging ghost accounts is found in court records from the city of Exeter, capital of the county of Devon in the southern part of England. The central figure in this tale was a fourteen-year-old boy named Richard Tarwell, who worked for the Harrises, a wealthy Devon family.

The head of the family, George Harris, held an important position in the king's court. He was often required to spend long periods in London away from his Devon estate. The property was left in the care of his butler, Richard Morris. Morris had been with the family for years and was considered completely trustworthy.

In 1730, George Harris was in London when he received an urgent letter from Morris, asking him to return at once. Harris managed to break off his government business and rush back to Devon. Morris met him and, with some anxiety, explained what had happened.

A few days earlier, Morris said, he had been awakened from a sound sleep by unexplained noises. He crept downstairs and heard, through the closed door off the butler's pantry, the sound of snapping wood, as if someone were breaking into the boxes in which the Harris family's valuable silver was stored. He also heard the voices of two men. At first Morris thought the robbers must be the two footmen, for he was sure that no one could have gotten into the house without breaking down a door; that would have made a great deal of noise and awakened the entire household.

Morris was so enraged by the thought that these two men had betrayed their employer that he burst into the butler's pantry without a thought for his own safety. Much to his surprise, Morris found the men breaking into the silver box were not the footmen, but two rough-looking men he had never seen before. And with the robbers was fourteen-year-old Richard Tarwell.

Tarwell was a lad Morris had hired just a few weeks earlier to help with the kitchen work. The boy's family lived in the area, and he seemed reliable enough when he started the job. He also appeared to enjoy his work. At night he slept in a small cubbyhole near the butler's pantry. Morris assumed that he had let the two robbers into the house.

The robbers immediately turned on Morris, beat him, tied and gagged him, and ran off. Morris was not discovered until the following morning, when the other servants wondered why the butler, habitually the most punctual of men, had not appeared for breakfast.

The butler was badly shaken but not seriously injured. It was at this point that Morris sent the letter to Harris, which brought the master of the house running from London.

After the robbery, no trace of the silver, the two

robbers, or Richard Tarwell could be found. Tarwell's father protested the boy's innocence; but without the boy there to tell his own side of the story his guilt was presumed.

George Harris took the loss of his silver philosophically. He said that his was not the first family to be robbed, and would not be the last. He returned to London to continue his work for the king, and it was several months before he could again go to his Devon estate.

No progress had been made in finding either the missing silver or those who had taken it. Harris had tried to dismiss the whole matter from his mind, but still he worried. On his first night back, he followed the butler around the house as the servant locked up. Harris marveled at the extraordinary care this trusted man took in locking and securing all the doors and windows. He had never before noticed how careful Morris was. He told his wife that Morris must be taking unusual precautions since the robbery. His wife, who had always been more attentive to domestic affairs, assured him that Morris habitually took such care.

As Harris retired to bed, something, he wasn't quite sure what, began to bother him. He tossed and turned for a while, trying to focus on what had troubled him, but finally he gave up and fell asleep.

He was sleeping soundly, yet in the middle of the

night, for a reason he was unable to explain, he was suddenly fully awake. By the light of a small lamp that he always kept burning near his bed, Harris saw a young boy standing at the foot of the bed. Though he had never seen the boy before, somehow he knew that this was the missing Richard Tarwell.

Harris' first thought was that the boy had somehow been hiding in the house in the months since the robbery. Harris asked him what he was doing, but the boy said nothing. He merely beckoned. The silence was puzzling. Harris then thought the boy might have received an injury to the throat, or perhaps some fright had deprived him of the ability to speak.

The figure of Richard Tarwell moved toward the door, beckoning Harris to follow. For some reason, he felt almost compelled to do so. He pulled on boots, threw a cloak over his nightclothes, and picked up his sword. Then he followed the boy.

As they crossed the hall, Harris noticed that the figure moved without making a sound. For the first time, he began to realize that the Richard Tarwell that stood in front of him was not a living boy at all. Yet strangely, he felt no fear. As he later stated, he was sure that the ghost meant him no harm.

The pair went downstairs and out a side door, which, Harris saw to his amazement, was unlocked. Yet he had watched Morris lock the door that very evening.

Once out of the house, the figure led Harris about one hundred yards toward a large oak, the trunk of which was surrounded, and almost hidden by a thick growth of low shrubs and bushes. At the tree the boy stopped and pointed to the ground. Then he walked around the far side of the tree and disappeared from view.

Harris called to him softly, but there was no answer. Since it would have been impossible for a living person to move through the thick tangle of underbrush without making a noise, and Harris heard nothing, this seemed proof positive that he had seen the ghost of Richard Tarwell. But in the darkness there was nothing more he could do. He returned to the house, locking the door behind him. He resolved that in the morning he must find out what the ghost had wanted of him.

Harris awakened with the first light of dawn. It would be more accurate to say that he got up with the first light of dawn, for after his experience he had hardly slept at all. As he lay awake he had conceived a plan. He went quietly to the room where the two footmen slept and roused them. He told the footmen to dress, find some spades, and come with him to the spot near the large oak tree.

Shortly after the footmen began digging at the spot the ghost had pointed out, they found shreds of mildewed cloth. They immediately recognized the cloth as having come from Richard Tarwell's coat. "And if I am not mistaken," Harris said, "his body will be in it." And indeed the boy's decaying remains were found very shortly.

Harris now knew what he had already begun to suspect: that his trusted butler, Morris, had committed the crime and that young Richard Tarwell had been its innocent victim. The question that had been nagging at Harris' mind before he went to bed and saw the ghost was: Where did Morris keep the keys with which he locked up the house? He now recalled that Morris kept all his keys in a drawer close to his bed. There were only two sets of keys; the butler had one and he had the other. Harris had his keys with him in London at the time of the robbery. In order for Richard Tarwell to have let anyone into the house, he would have had to steal the keys from Morris' room without waking him. This would have been a difficult, if not impossible, task, particularly since Morris admitted that he was a light sleeper who had been awakened by sounds coming from the floor below.

Harris sent one of the footmen for the constables, and when they arrived Morris was accused of the crime. At first he denied everything, but when he was taken to the spot where Richard Tarwell had been buried he broke down and confessed. He had let the two men in. They were his accomplices. While they were breaking into the box containing the silver, the boy had been awakened (he slept nearby) and surprised them. One of the men attacked Richard Tarwell and killed him. Then all three buried his body near the oak. Murder had not been part of the original plan, and at first Morris and his accomplices did not know what to do. Then they hit upon the idea of tying Morris up and trying to pin the blame for the robbery on the missing boy.

The plan would have worked, if Richard Tarwell himself had not come back from the dead to expose it and clear his name.

Morris' accomplices were to have taken the silver to Plymouth, sold it, and sent the butler his share. But they double-crossed him and were never heard from again. Nor was any trace of the stolen silver ever found.

Morris alone suffered for the crime. He was hanged. At least he is the only one that we know of who was punished. Perhaps Richard Tarwell's avenging ghost tracked down the other two as well.

*Henry Sidgwick,
first president of the
Society for Psychical
Research*

*Frederic Myers,
one of the founders
of the Society for
Psychical Research*

THREE

Ghost Hunters' Stories

NEAR THE END OF THE NINETEENTH century, a group of intelligent and dedicated English men and women got together to form the world's first scientific ghost-hunting society. They called themselves the Society for Psychical Research (S.P.R.), and since they were very serious people they probably would not like to be called "ghost hunters." But in many respects that's just what they were. They collected, and investigated, what we would call ghost stories.

People had collected, told, and retold ghost stories for centuries. But the founders of the S.P.R. were not just collectors of folklore or spooky old tales. They thought that such accounts might supply some solid clues that would help answer the question of whether the spirit survives bodily death. Therefore, they were not content just to write down what somebody told them. They tried to check out the information and apply scientific discipline to their collecting.

Their task was not an easy one, and often the researchers fell short of their goals. But even the harshest critics of psychical research would have to admit that the founders of the S.P.R. had made an honest attempt. No one had ever tried to collect and investigate such accounts before, so there was a wealth of uncollected material to draw on. And no later investigators ever did a better job.

Children figure prominently in a fair number of the early S.P.R. cases, either as "ghosts" or "percipients," that is, the individuals who see or otherwise experience the supernatural event.

In the next few pages we are going to look back at that ghostly golden age by reviewing some of the cases found in the early files of the S.P.R.

WORLD WAR I PROVIDED an enormous number of accounts for the S.P.R. The war, with its great slaughter of young men, made the British public acutely conscious of sudden death, and yearn more than ever to find hope of survival after death.

Many people wrote to the S.P.R. telling them how they had become aware of the death of a loved one on the battlefield by supernatural means, long before they could have learned by any normal means.

A LETTER FROM A Mrs. E. S. Russell tells a typical story. Her husband was killed in France on November 6, 1917. Communications being what they were, she did not learn of the death for another ten days. At about the time he was killed (she was not sure of the exact date or time), she was sitting with her son, Dicky, aged about three-and-one-half years.

Mother and son were talking when "he sat up rather suddenly and said, 'Daddy is dead.' I said, 'Oh, no, dear, he's not and I expect he'll come back to us someday'; but Dicky looked very upset and became flushed and almost wept and said again, 'No, he won't. Dick knows he's dead.' I just said, 'No, dear, I don't think he is,' but Dicky seemed so distressed and repeated, 'No, no, Dick knows it' so emphatically that I thought best to leave the subject alone. He never referred to it again and had never said anything of the sort before."

Mrs. Russell said the incident was so odd that she told her sister about it. She also insisted that at the time she had no particular anxiety about her husband's safety. He had been through a number of difficult engagements without a scratch, and she had gotten used to the idea of danger.

Mrs. Russell's sister confirmed the account.

ANOTHER WORLD WAR I CASE is the interesting and complex series of events which surrounded the death of Captain Eldred Bowyer-Bower. He was a twenty-two-year-old pilot killed in action on March 19, 1917. Three persons, in three widely scattered places, appear to have received a strong intimation of his death at about the time it occurred, and long before they could have known of it through any natural means.

The most remarkable of these experiences was reported by Captain Bowyer-Bower's half-sister, Mrs. Spearman, who was in India at the time of his death. She was sitting with her newborn baby on the morning of March 19 when:

"I had a great feeling I must turn round and did, to see Eldred; he looked so happy and that dear mischievous look. I was so glad to see him, and told him I would just put baby in a safer place, then we could talk. 'Fancy coming out here,' I said, turning round again, and was just putting my hands out to give him a hug and a kiss, but Eldred was gone. I called and looked for him. I never saw him again."

At about the same time, the "ghost" of Captain Bowyer-Bower was also seen by his niece, a child about three years old. The incident was described in a letter to the S.P.R. by Mrs. Cecily Chater, the girl's mother.

"One morning while I was still in bed, about 9:15, she came into my room and said, 'Uncle Alley Boy is downstairs,' [Alley Boy was a family pet name for the captain] and although I told her he was in France, she insisted that she had seen him. Later in the day I happened to be writing to my mother and mentioned this, not because I thought much about it, but to show that Betty still thought and spoke of her uncle of whom she was very fond. A few days afterwards we found the date my brother was missing was the date on the letter . . . The child was a little under three years old at the time . . . I have never attached much importance to this incident as it may be just only a childish lie."

Perhaps that is all it was, but considering it happened at the time that the captain was killed, it is a strange coincidence. Combined with Mrs. Spearman's experience, the coincidence becomes stranger still.

The third experience does not involve an actual sighting, but rather a feeling of doom. The captain's mother received a letter from a Mrs. Watson, an elderly lady she had known for many years. Mrs. Watson had not written for about eighteen months, and then quite unexpectedly came a letter saying, "Something tells me you are having great anxiety about Eldred.

Will you let me know?" The letter was dated March 19, 1917, the day the captain was killed. But at the time his mother knew nothing of this. She wrote back to Mrs. Watson asking why she had this feeling of concern about Eldred. Mrs. Watson replied that on the afternoon of the day she wrote her letter she had an awful feeling that he had been killed.

The image of Captain Bowyer-Bower was also reported to have appeared to several other people. But this was after his death became known to them. His spirit was also reputedly contacted by several spirit mediums.

A VERY STRANGE WORLD WAR I story was supplied to the S.P.R. by Mrs. Ellen Jones. Early in the morning of July 26, 1916, Mrs. Jones was awakened from a deep sleep with the distinct impression that someone was in her room.

"I opened my eyes to absolute darkness, but at the right side of my bed stood a misty figure, which I at first took for my little grandson, and I asked him why he was there. No answer came, but the face became more distinct, and I saw it resembled a photograph of my son-in-law, taken when he was about three years old. In the photograph one can see short curls, but in my vision the lower part of the forehead, eyebrows, eyes, nose, mouth, and part of the chin were clearly visible, but hair, ears, lower part of chin and neck were hidden by white wrappings [bandages]. As I looked and wondered, the mouth expanded into a smile and the appearance vanished, the room being still in darkness."

Mrs. Jones was alarmed at first, thinking that something might have happened to her grandson. The boy was quite well, but her son-in-law, Lieutenant G.E.W. Bridge, was at that very moment lying in a military hospital at Boulogne, with his head bandaged exactly as in Mrs. Jones' vision. Mrs. Jones, however, did not know at the time that her son-in-law had been wounded.

Lieutenant Bridge recovered from his wounds, and he was the one who brought the incident to the attention of the S.P.R.; so this is not, strictly speaking, a ghost story. But it a very strange event nevertheless.

A MORE TRADITIONAL ghostly encounter can be found in the experience of the four young Du Cane sisters. On the night of November 1, 1889, they had gone up to their bedrooms at about 10:00 P.M. The girls slept in two adjoining bedrooms, but all four had gone into one of the rooms in order to find some matches to light the gas lamp. The eldest of them, Louisa Du Cane, wrote:

"There was no light beyond that which glimmered through the venetian blinds in each room. As I stood by the mantlepiece, I was awe-struck by the sudden appearance of a figure gliding noiselessly towards me from the outer room. The appearance was that of a young man, of middle height, dressed in dark clothes, and wearing a peaked cap. His face was very pale, and his eyes downcast as though in deep thought. His mouth was shaded by a dark moustache. The face was slightly luminous, which enabled us to distinguish the features distinctly, although we were without a light of any kind at the time.

"The apparition glided onwards towards my sisters, who were standing inside the room, quite close to the outer door, and who had first caught sight of it reflected in the mirror. When within a few inches of them it vanished as suddenly as it appeared. As the figure passed we distinctly felt a cold air which seemed to accompany it. We have never seen it again, and cannot account in any way for the phenomenon."

Mrs. Eleanor M. Sidgwick, an investigator for the S.P.R. (and wife of the group's first president), visited the Du Cane girls. She questioned them, examined the room in which the experience was supposed to have taken place, and could find no reason for doubting the truth of their tale.

A TRAGIC TALE WAS RELATED to the S.P.R. by Annie Wright, the wife of a railway inspector. It took place on the afternoon of May 17, 1879. (The S.P.R. did not receive a report on this case until 1883, because in 1879 there was no S.P.R. It was founded in 1882.) Mrs. Wright had just let her little girl go out and play.

"As I was walking across the yard the child came in front of me like a bright shadow, and I stopped quite still and looked at her, and turned my head to the right, and saw her pass away. I emptied my water bucket, and was coming in. My husband's brother, who was staying with us, called to me and said, 'Fanny have got runned over.' "

Mrs. Wright rushed to the road where she found her daughter had been knocked down by a baker's cart. The child was still alive when she arrived, but others at the scene of the accident heard Mrs. Wright say, "This is her deathblow. I saw her shadow in the yard." The girl died in her mother's arms.

THIS IS JUST the tiniest sampling of the huge number of cases collected by members of the S.P.R. during that extraordinary early period. It is easy enough to pick holes in them as proof of psychic phenomena. Critics have done so very effectively for a long time now. The difficulty of building a conclusive case for survival of bodily death turned out to be far more difficult than the pioneers of psychical research had imagined. Nevertheless, these cases remain a unique, compelling, and rather spooky record of one area of human experience.

FOUR

Rosalie

HAVE YOU EVER HEARD OF A LITTLE GIRL ghost called Rosalie? I would be very much surprised if you have. Nearly sixty years ago, Rosalie was, for a brief time, the most famous child ghost in the world. Her luster has been dimmed by time, but we will get to all of that. Famous or not, the case of little Rosalie is still a good one, and is still rather mysterious.

The story of Rosalie really begins with a man named Harry Price. From the early 1920s until his death in 1948, Harry Price was one of Britain's leading psychical researchers. He was certainly the most effective and best-known publicist of ghostly investigations, and was widely known by the title "The Ghost

Hunter." He had reported many strange experiences in his life, but none stranger than Rosalie.

Dr. Paul Tabori, who compiled an official biography of Price, said:

> "But he had at least one experience which shook him and moved him deeply—an experience that remains a complete enigma to this day. It is known as the Rosalie case. When I began to sift through Harry Price's papers, it was one of the first manuscripts of his I came upon, and once I read it I continued to search for details or unpublished evidence with growing excitement. I must confess that I have found practically nothing. Rosalie has disappeared into thin air and no trace of her meeting with Harry Price remains except his own account and a few chance references to her in his letters."

Tabori believed that Price had been so shaken by his experience that he absolutely declined to say any more about it. Nor did anyone else step forward to add any details, despite many appeals.

Here is the story as Harry Price told it. On the morning of December 8, 1937, Price was telephoned by a lady who said she knew of his psychical research work and had been impressed. She wanted him to attend a private séance at her house at which the spirit of a little girl named Rosalie always materialized. However, Price was made to promise that he would never reveal the identity of any of those who attended the séance or the place in which it was held. The family wanted absolutely no publicity, out of fear that the spirit might be frightened away.

Those who attend séances are often sensitive about publicity, so Price was not surprised by this request, and agreed. On Wednesday, December 15, 1937, Harry Price went to what he called "one of the better-class London suburbs."

He was admitted to a large mid-Victorian house by a parlor maid, shortly after 7:00 P.M. Inside he met Mr. and Mrs. X, as Price called them, and their daughter, aged about seventeen. Over supper he was told the story of Rosalie.

A friend of Mrs. X, a Frenchwoman Price referred to as Mme. Z, had married an English officer at the beginning of World War I. The officer was killed in 1916, leaving his wife with an infant daughter, Rosalie. The daughter was not destined to survive long; she died of diphtheria, a common childhood disease, in 1921.

Some five years after her daughter's death, Mme. Z began to sense the presence of her daughter's spirit. The feeling grew stronger, and after some months she heard Rosalie's voice call out "Mother." As the manifestation grew even stronger, Mme. Z was not only able to see the spirit of her daughter but was actually able to grasp her hand.

Mme. Z discussed these events with Mr. and Mrs. X, who apparently had a previous interest in spiritualism and psychic phenomena. They suggested that regular séances be held at their house in order to summon the spirit of Rosalie. These séances began in the spring of 1929, and continued more or less regularly on Wednesday evenings up until the time that Price was called in. Usually in attendance at the séances were only Mr. and Mrs. X, their daughter, and Mme. Z, though an occasional outsider was admitted. Rosalie appeared at almost every séance.

After dinner Price was taken into the room in which the séance was to be held, and introduced to Mme. Z and another sitter, a young man whom Price called Jim. He was also introduced to another servant in the house, the cook.

Fraud was common at séances. Even those deeply convinced of the reality of the spirit world recognized this fact. Harry Price had attended many séances and was well aware of the possibility of a hoax.

He had been told that he would not be allowed to bring a light into the séance room, or speak to or touch the spirit unless given permission to do so. But no other restrictions were placed on him. He examined the entire house, and paid particular attention to the séance room itself. He locked the door and put the key in his pocket. He then sealed all the doors and windows with adhesive tape and initialed the tape.

He spread powder in front of the fireplace, in order to detect footprints of anyone coming or going that way.

When he was convinced the room was completely sealed from the outside, he began a minute examination of the inside: opening all the drawers, looking under the rugs, and so forth. He found nothing in the least suspicious. He examined the clothing of Jim and Mr. X, but then he faced a problem, for he felt he "could not very well search the three ladies." Still he was convinced that they were concealing nothing on their persons.

Shortly after 9:00 P.M., the séance was finally ready to begin. The six people sat in a circle of chairs in the middle of the room. Mr. X switched off the light, and for about twenty minutes they chatted quietly in total darkness. Then Mr. X turned on the radio to provide some music. The illuminated panel of the radio also threw off enough light for Price to see the others in the room dimly, but well enough to make out their individual features. After a short time, Mr. X switched off the radio and told the sitters to remain absolutely silent. Mme. Z began to call "Rosalie?" and she sobbed softly.

A few minutes later Mrs. X whispered, "Rosalie is here—don't speak." Price sensed the presence of something in the room. There was also an unusual but not an unpleasant smell. There was a sound like the shuffling of feet, and something warm and soft touched his hand. He heard Mme. Z whispering softly to the child.

So far, all of the manifestations were fairly common séance-room phenomena. Price must have had similar experiences many times before. What happened next was not at all common. Price asked if he could touch the materialization, and he was given permission to do so. Price stretched out his hand and touched what he took to be the nude figure of a little girl of about six. Her long hair fell about her shoulders. He took her right hand and felt her pulse; it was about ninety beats a minute. He put his ear to her chest and heard her heartbeat.

Plaques covered with a substance that glowed in the dark and cast a dim greenish light had been placed in the séance room, and at this point it was agreed that they should be used. The light cast by these luminous plaques revealed what Price called "a beautiful child who would have graced any nursery in the land."

Price was allowed to ask Rosalie a short series of questions about how she spent her time in the spirit world, but she did not answer any of the questions. He then asked the phantom if she loved her mother. Rosalie "lisped 'yes.' " Mme. Z hugged the little girl,

Left:
An artist's sketch of the house in which the Rosalie séance was supposed to have been held.

Right:
A sketch of the séance room. The X on the floor marks the spot where the spirit of Rosalie is said to have appeared.

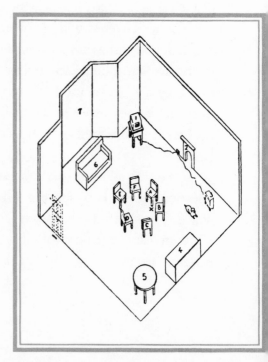

and Mrs. X said that the luminous plaques should be covered. By this time the women were sobbing loudly, and Price himself was deeply moved. The séance ended at about eleven o'clock.

When the lights were turned back on, Price reexamined all the seals and the powder. Things were exactly as he had left them before the séance began. He again took a quick tour of the remainder of the house to see if anything was amiss. He could find nothing out of the ordinary. Convinced he had taken every possible precaution to prevent fraud, Harry Price left the house, went straight to his London club, and proceeded to write his report.

In 1939 this report appeared in his book *Fifty Years of Psychical Research*. Naturally it created a sensation, and was widely quoted or republished in newspapers and magazines of the time.

There were many unique and impressive features of the Rosalie story. While materializations, or alleged materializations, were common séance-room phenomena, they usually took place under such poorly controlled conditions that the "spirit" could easily have been (and often turned out to be) the medium or an assistant wrapped in a sheet. A medium is a person who is supposed to have special powers to contact the spirits of the dead.

But here the séance took place in what amounted to a sealed room. No one in that room could possibly have impersonated a six-year-old girl. Nor could a projector or some other illusion have been used. Price not only saw the ghost, he felt her pulse. And there was something else; most spiritualistic frauds had been stimulated by greed. Someone wanted to make money. But as Price pointed out:

"No one was getting anything out of it. Neither money nor publicity nor kudos. And would any sane family fool one another every week for years on end? Hardly! And where did the spirit come from? Was there a revolving wall in the drawing room or a trapdoor in the very solid parquet floor? If so, could it have survived my minute and systematic search of the apartment? I suppose that is possible but moving floors and sliding walls imply costly, elaborate, and silent machinery to operate. And what could possibly be the motive for such a stupendous fraud?"

He added that a band of highly skilled actors would also have been necessary.

In the many months between the event itself, and the publication of his account, Harry Price described the Rosalie séance to only one other person. This person was Mrs. K. M. Goldney, another researcher and sometime associate of Price. The day after the séance, Mrs. Goldney dropped by Price's office. She reported that he looked shaken and haggard. She had never seen him look worse. His slight stutter had become more pronounced as he gave her an emotional description of the séance.

Mrs. Goldney was impressed. She wanted Price to forget the assurances of anonymity he had given and continue his investigations. She even suggested that he bring the Archbishop of Canterbury to Mr. and Mrs. X to tell them "the happiness of the whole human race is affected and they MUST allow further investigation."

But Price stood firm on his promise. Later Price reported that at the end of August, 1939, Mr. X took his family for an automobile tour of the Continent. Mme. Z went with them as far as Paris, where she was to visit her French relatives. The war broke out and the X family was unable to get back to Paris to pick up Rosalie's mother. They barely escaped themselves. Nothing more was ever heard from Mme. Z.

A sad and disappointing ending to a most sensational case. But that did nothing to dim its popularity. However, at about the same time as the Rosalie incident, Price began the series of investigations at a haunted house called Borley Rectory which were to make him more famous than ever. There is no place for a discussion of Borley here—it involves no child ghosts. But the details were so sensational that the Borley case soon eclipsed Rosalie and everything else in Harry Price's long career in psychical research. Up to the time of his death in 1948, Borley remained

Students visiting Borley Rectory, site of a sensational haunting investigated by Harry Price.

Price's chief claim to fame, and to whatever fortune he could obtain from two best-selling books on the subject. Rosalie was forgotten.

While Rosalie had been a great, if temporary, popular success, not all of Harry Price's serious psychical research colleagues were impressed. They freely admitted that there was little chance that Price could have been deceived in a fraudulent séance. He was far too experienced for that. What they doubted was whether the séance had taken place at all. There was not one single other witness ready to step forward to support Price's tale.

Eric Dingwall, who had developed a reputation of being a gadfly to other researchers, wrote Price a caustic letter.

"I see your after-dinner story of the materialization has had a wide publicity. It seems very odd that you never told me a word about this miracle, if it occurred. It is also very odd that in all these remarkable tales there are no names, addresses, or means of checking. I have another one now. One of the most eminent lawyers in the provinces tells me that at a séance at which he was present (no details, of course) a white horse materialized and walked round the circle. I will suggest to him that your circle should meet his and that we should be treated to the first materialized Lady Godiva. . . . What is the real object of telling these tales?"

The only bit of confirming evidence came from Mrs. Goldney. No one ever doubted her integrity, but she had not attended the séance. All she could recount was what Price had told her, and her impression that Price was in an extremely emotional state the morning after the experience.

In the months and years that followed, no one who could supply additional information was discovered. Mme. Z had disappeared in France, which was then occupied by the Germans. Perhaps she died there. Mr. and Mrs. X may still have felt bound by the promise of silence. Perhaps they just did not want the publicity. But what about Jim, who had attended the séance with Price, or one of the small number of others who had been privileged to see the spirit? What about the parlor maid or the cook or the other servants who may have worked in the house? What about people Mr. and Mrs. X or the other sitters or the servants may have talked to? Sensational secrets like this are hard to keep. But for poor Rosalie there was a wall of silence.

The end of the story sounds a bit suspicious as well. Why would Mr. X have taken his family and Mme. Z to the Continent in August, 1939, for a tour? Everyone with a grain of sense knew that war was going to break out at any moment and that such a trip would be filled with danger. It is all too convenient.

Then there was the discouraging lack of additional information in Price's voluminous papers. Had he jotted down anything from which more information could be obtained? Apparently he did not.

At this point you and I might be inclined to write the whole thing off as a Harry Price hoax, and leave it at that. But some psychical researchers are unbelievably dogged. They will not rest until every possible avenue has been explored. Eric Dingwall, as was already noted, had been skeptical of Rosalie from the first. Along with an equally skeptical colleague, Trevor Hall, he decided to reexamine all the available evidence. Investigations like this are not undertaken to disprove the possibility of ghosts or of survival after death. Most of those who engage in psychical research are deeply committed to such beliefs.

By the mid-1950s the researchers had abandoned hope that any of those who could shed more light on the Rosalie story would step forward voluntarily. But there did seem to be one promising lead. Price had given a fairly full description of the exterior of the house in which the séance had taken place. Among his papers was found a note which the researchers regarded as proof that the séance had taken place in the south London district known as Brockley.

Dingwall and Hall obtained detailed maps of Brockley and surrounding districts. After hours of poring over these maps, they could find only one house which seemed to fit the description given by Price. But upon visiting that house they found a number of important variations from the Price description. One of the most significant was that the house had changed hands between 1929 and 1937. Thus the séances could not have been conducted only in that house as Price had indicated. Dingwall and Hall concluded, "It seems safe to say, therefore, that there appears to be no house in Brockley which complies with the description given by Price . . . and that this description must therefore be regarded as probably fictitious."

The researchers discovered, however, that as a young man, Price had attended a number of séances in houses in Brockley during which materializations of spirits were supposed to have taken place. Dingwall and Hall speculate that Price had drawn on some early memories in putting together the Rosalie story.

But why would he have done it? That, of course, we can never know. If he had made up the story, it was a bold and dangerous act which could have jeopardized his entire career in psychical research. He surely knew that such a dramatic tale would come under intense scrutiny; and if he couldn't come up with confirming evidence, he would eventually suffer.

Dingwall and Hall point out that in 1937, Price's reputation was already in jeopardy. Some years earlier he had a falling-out with many of his psychical research colleagues. The National Laboratory of Psychical Research, which Price founded, then collapsed from lack of financial support. The public no longer seemed interested in Harry Price. He might have believed that an exciting story like Rosalie was what he needed to recapture public attention.

But the skepticism and downright disbelief of other psychical researchers must have given him pause. Besides, his Borley Rectory investigations had already begun to create a sensation, and his reputation was on the rise again. (Incidentally, Dingwall, Hall, and Mrs. Goldney looked into Price's Borley work as well, and found it full of contradictions and misrepresentations of fact.)

There is some indication that by 1941 Price had begun to regret that he had ever brought up the Rosalie story in the first place. He stopped talking about the little girl ghost, though he never admitted that the incident had never taken place.

That is the story of Rosalie. Despite momentary fame, it turned out that the evidence in the case was not nearly as good as it first sounded. This is a good story to keep in mind the next time you read of some "ghost hunter" who says he has met, face to face, with this or that spirit.

FIVE
Reverend Wesley's Poltergeist

THERE IS NO GHOSTLY PHENOMENON more closely associated with children than the poltergeist. The word is German, and means noisy or rattling ghost or spirit. In one form or another, poltergeists have been reported for centuries.

In a typical poltergeist case, a house is suddenly afflicted with a series of strange and unexplainable noises—banging, rattling, scratching, and the like. Objects may be moved or even thrown about. Small objects have been reported flying clear across a room, while large pieces of furniture slide along the floor. Sometimes a shower of stones, or what sounds like a shower of stones, is thrown at a window or roof. In most cases there are no voices or apparitions; but as we shall see, it is not possible to generalize.

Usually the phenomena are considered harmless, except, of course, to the nerves of those living in the afflicted house. But occasionally poltergeist activity may turn violent, causing a good deal of damage and even injuries. The safest thing you can say about poltergeists is that they are unpredictable.

Many different theories have been advanced to explain poltergeist activity. Some say the poltergeist is a mindless or mischievous spirit. The activity generally seems to be rather pointless. Others think the poltergeist is an impersonal but powerful "psychic force" which is triggered by the presence of a sensitive or susceptible individual. Yet another explanation is that poltergeists are a combination of natural events, trickery, and an active imagination, and that there is nothing psychic or supernatural about them.

Investigating poltergeist cases took up a good deal of the time and energy of early psychical researchers. Even today good poltergeist cases are far and away the most common of the reported ghostly events.

That is all well and good, you say, but what does it have to do with children? Plenty. Anyone who has even a casual knowledge of the history of poltergeists knows that in a huge majority of these cases, the phenomena—the noises, the moving objects—seem to center around the young, generally boys or girls between the ages of about ten and nineteen. This fact is so striking that there are many suggestions as to why.

Two theories predominate. First, that there is something in the psychic makeup of children which triggers the phenomena. Second, that making strange noises and throwing objects about are just the sort of tricks children would play.

The most forceful statement of this second point of view was made by the pioneer psychical researcher Frank Podmore:

"1. We have positive evidence, by confession or detection, or both, that in some cases tricky little girls or boys have thrown about crockery and upset the kitchen furniture with their own hands, whilst the on-lookers have accepted the portent as a manifestation of supernormal powers.

"2. We have, speaking broadly, no good evidence of anything having been done which could not have been done by a girl or boy of slightly more than the average cunning and naughtiness."

Podmore concluded:

"In no case that I have yet seen recorded has any adequate or intelligible motive beyond that of mere childish vanity and love of excitement been assigned for the performance."

Not all psychical researchers would agree with Podmore's judgment. Most probably would not, but few would disagree that childish trickery does play a large part in the phenomena.

While there have been hundreds and hundreds of poltergeist cases recorded and investigated, the disturbances which took place in the Parsonage at Epworth, England, in December and January, 1716–17 are among the best known and most thoroughly investigated. The reason for all the attention is that the Parsonage at Epworth was the birthplace of John Wesley, founder of Methodism and one of the most influential religious leaders of the eighteenth century.

John Wesley himself was not a direct witness to the strange phenomena, but many members of his large family were. Wesley retained an interest in the events throughout his life, and he always seemed to believe that some spiritual or diabolical force was involved in them.

Toward the end of 1716, the house was afflicted by a variety of strange and inexplicable noises— knocks and rumblings—which reverberated from cellar to attic.

Writing to her eldest son, Mrs. Wesley described some of the events:

"One night it made such a noise in the room over our heads as if several people were walking; then run

The Reverend John Wesley, whose family members were
afflicted by the strange activity of a poltergeist.

up and down stairs, and was so outrageous, that we thought the children would be frightened, so your father and I rose and went down in the dark to light a candle. Just as we came to the bottom of the broad stairs, having hold of each other, on my side there seemed as if somebody had emptied a bag of money at my feet, and on his as if all the bottles under the stairs (which were many) had been dashed in a thousand pieces. We passed through the hall into the kitchen and got a candle and went to see the children. The next night your father would get Mr. Hoole [a neighbor] to lie at our house, and we all sat together till one or two o'clock in the morning, and heard the knocking as usual. Sometimes it would make a noise like the winding up of a jack; at other times, as that night Mr. Hoole was with us, like a carpenter planing deals; but most commonly it knocked thrice and stopped and then thrice again, and so many hours together."

Often when Reverend Wesley, John's father, tapped his stick on the floor, the poltergeist would answer with knocks of its own. The poltergeist even disturbed this pious family at its prayers. It became particularly unruly when the names of King George I and the prince were mentioned in a prayer. Reverend Wesley tried to speak to it, but never received any replies, "only once or twice two or three feeble squeaks, a little louder than the chirping of a bird, but not like the noise of rats which I have often heard."

Wesley remained defiant, calling the poltergeist, "thou deaf and dumb devil."

Sometimes door latches seemed to rise mysteriously, and Wesley recorded, "I have been thrice pushed by an invisible power, once against the corner of my desk in the study, a second time against the door of the matted chamber, a third time against the right side of the frame of my study door as I was going in."

Some strange things were seen, but they were certainly not the traditional ghost. Mrs. Wesley reported seeing under her bed, "like a badger only without any head that was discernible." One of the hired men saw something that looked like a white rabbit, but not quite.

According to Mrs. Wesley, "One night when the noise was great in the kitchen . . . and the door in the yard, the latch whereof was often lifted up, my daughter Emilia went and held it fast on the inside, but it was lifted up, and the door pushed violently against her though nothing was to be seen on the outside."

The Wesleys got a dog in an attempt to track down or frighten away whatever it was that was causing all the disturbances. That didn't work. In fact, the noises frightened the dog. The Wesley children, however, did not seem at all frightened once they got used to the noises. Indeed, they actually seemed to enjoy the excitement created by the poltergeist. They dubbed it "Old Jeffrey," after someone who had died in the house. In their accounts they often speak of "Old Jeffrey" in a very friendly manner.

After about two months the mysterious phenomena simply faded away, though the family continued to discuss and even write about the happenings for many years. As late as 1786, John Wesley published an article on the subject. Upon John's death, all of the materials that he had collected—his own father's firsthand account, letters written by family members at the time and later, and statements made by servants or others in the household—were published.

In his book *Ghosts and Hauntings*, author Dennis Bardens declares flatly, "There is absolutely nothing in the lives of this worthy, God-fearing family to support even a suspicion that they could or would be capable of fraud." But others who have examined the case are not quite so sure.

Psychical researcher Frank Podmore went over the evidence relating to the case. He found that all of the firsthand contemporary accounts, that is, the statements written shortly after the events had taken place, by people who had actually been there, concerned strange noises, broken objects, and other relatively unspectacular events.

Secondhand accounts, and those taken from witnesses months or years later, were generally much more impressive. These accounts were filled with difficult-to-explain events, like doors being mysteriously thrown open while someone was trying to hold them closed. Podmore concludes that the Wesley family was engaging in the inevitable human tendency to exaggerate.

By picking and choosing among the various narratives, the events at Epworth Parsonage can be made to sound incredible indeed. If only the contemporary firsthand accounts are used, a different picture emerges.

What may be most significant about the accounts collected by John Wesley is the one that isn't there —a statement by one of the elder Wesley girls, Hetty. Hetty would have been about nineteen at the time and fully capable of writing out her experiences, but for some reason she never seemed to, or at least her account has never been made public.

This is all the more curious since many of the disturbances seemed to center around Hetty. Not only was she always on the spot when there were strange noises, she often behaved oddly as well.

Mrs. Wesley wrote:

> "All the family, as well as Robin, were asleep when your father and I went downstairs, nor did they wake in the nursery when we held the candle close by them, only we observed that Hetty trembled exceedingly in her sleep, as she always did before the noise awakened her. It commonly was nearer her than the rest."

Then there is this extract from the letter of another Wesley sister, Emily:

"No sooner was I got upstairs, and undressing for bed, but I heard a noise among many bottles that stand under the stairs, just like the throwing of a great stone among them, which had broken them all to pieces. This made me hasten to bed; but my sister Hetty, who sits always to wait on my father going to bed, was still sitting on the lowest step of the garret stairs."

Or from another of Emily's letters:

"It [the noise] never followed me as it did my sister Hetty. I have been with her when it has knocked under her, and when she has moved, it has followed and still kept just under her feet."

There is a good deal more like this in the evidence for the Epworth poltergeist. That is why it is exceptionally unfortunate and frankly suspicious that we do not have Hetty's own description of what happened.

Was Hetty just a young hoaxer, as so many others have been? Or did something truly odd happen in the Wesley household back in 1716–1717 that just happened to center around the unfortunate Hetty? The better part of three centuries has passed since these events took place. It is unlikely that new evidence one way or another will ever be found. As with so many ghostly accounts, this one is surrounded by a fog of uncertainty.

Charles Bailey Bell, descendant of John Bell, who was tormented by the Bell Witch of Tennessee.

SIX

The Bell Witch

THE BELL WITCH IS ONE OF THE MOST famous ghostly accounts in American history. But that name is a little confusing. In the first place, the events started out as a standard poltergeist case. But it did a lot of unpoltergeist-like things. For example, it talked. Once it got going it was downright gabby. So it could easily be classed as a ghost or spirit or called a haunting. It certainly was not a witch. But because people were not supposed to believe in ghosts, but were allowed to believe in witches, that is what it was called. And the name has stuck. You can call it what you wish. One thing everyone agrees on is that it's a strange and sinister tale.

The story of the Bell Witch began in 1817 on the farm of John Bell in Robertson County, Tennessee. This part of Tennessee was no longer frontier country in 1817, but most families still lived in isolated farmhouses. The Bell family—mother, father, four sons, and a daughter—lived in a plain two-story farmhouse. A small number of slaves lived in outbuildings. Two older children had already married, but did not live far away. The Bells were considered to be moderately prosperous and were well liked by their neighbors.

The disturbances began slowly. There were strange noises, the rappings and scratchings typical of poltergeist cases. At about this time John Bell reported seeing a strange animal. It looked like a dog, yet it didn't look like a dog. He got his gun and took a shot at it, but he missed. There was also something that looked like a turkey or some other large bird near the house. It too escaped. The noises got worse.

More ominous manifestations began. The thing was growing physically violent. At first, it simply pulled covers off beds. Then, according to an account written many years later by Richard Williams Bell, the youngest member of the family, it began "slapping people on the face, especially those who resisted the action of pulling the cover from the bed, and those who came as detectives to expose the trick. The blows were heard distinctly, like the open palm of a heavy hand, while the sting was keenly felt, and it did not neglect to pull my hair, and make Joel [another son] squeal as often." But the chief target of the witch seemed (at this stage anyway) to be Betsy—Elizabeth Bell—the one girl in the family, who at the time was about twelve years old.

At first the family tried to keep the strange events secret, not too difficult a task when there were no near neighbors. But as the witch's activities continued and grew worse, secrecy became more difficult. When invited to a neighbor's house for dinner, John Bell barely talked or ate. Later he explained, "All of a sudden my tongue became strangely affected. Something that felt like a fungus growth came on both sides, pressing against my jaws, filling my mouth so that I could not eat or talk."

Finally, the Bells were driven to ask for help. They called in James Johnson, a neighbor, friend, and a man known for his great piety and vigor as a lay preacher. Johnson visited the Bell farm, heard some of the noises, and decided that there was an evil presence at work. He returned with a committee of local residents whose job was to find out if this was a hoax. The committee decided it wasn't. But they didn't know what was going on. So they called the thing a witch.

As news of the Bell Witch spread, more people came to help, or just because they were curious. The witch seemed to be flattered by all the attention, and redoubled its efforts. The witch, incidentally, was always referred to as *it*. It began answering questions, first by means of a rapping code (one rap for yes, two raps for no, that sort of thing). Then slowly but surely it acquired the ability to speak. That marked yet another leap forward in the power of the Bell Witch.

According to the principal account of the Bell Witch, "It commenced whistling when spoken to, in a low broken sound, as if trying to speak in a whistling voice, and in this way it progressed, developing until the whistling sound was changed to a weak, flattering whisper, uttering indistinct words. The voice, however, gradually gained strength in articulating, and soon the utterances became distinct in a low whisper, so as to be understood in the absence of any other noise."

The witch's voice got louder and more persistent until it could be heard shrieking about the house at practically any time of the day or night.

Naturally the first question that everyone wanted the witch to answer was who or what it was. To this the witch gave several contradictory replies.

"I am a spirit from everywhere. Heaven, Hell, the Earth. I'm in the air, in houses, any place at any time. I've been created millions of years. That is all I will tell you." It then went on to give other answers.

"I am the spirit of a person who was buried in the woods nearby, and the grave has been disturbed, my bones disinterred and scattered, and one of my teeth was lost under this house. I'm here looking for that tooth." That is the traditional troubled spirit type of haunting, though a lost tooth seems rather a petty matter for a ghost.

Though the Bells were not supposed to believe in ghosts, they had undoubtedly heard of this sort of incident. They knew that there had been an Indian burial ground near their house, and they spent a lot of time digging around looking for the missing tooth until the witch declared that it had all been a joke.

Then there was another explanation. "I am the spirit of an early immigrant who brought a large sum of money and buried my treasure for safekeeping until needed. In the meanwhile I died without divulging the secret and I have returned in the spirit for the purpose of making known the hiding place. I want Betsy Bell to have the money."

This sent the Bell family off on another wild-goose chase. On the witch's instructions, they dug a huge rock out of a field. It was a task that involved hours of backbreaking labor, but nothing was found. The voice laughed at them for being so easily taken in by another lie.

The explanation which most caught the attention of the people of Robertson County was the witch's assertion that "I am nothing more nor less than old Kate Batts' witch . . ." Now Kate Batts was a local woman with a loud voice, foul temper, and something of a grudge against John Bell. She may have had a reputation as a witch, though she was also known for her endless and tedious quoting of Scripture. From then on, many people referred to the Bell Witch as Kate.

The problem with the identification was that Kate Batts was very much alive at the time. While people may have gossiped about her somehow or another being responsible for all the Bell family troubles, it is doubtful if many took that explanation very seriously. Kate Batts was never attacked by the Bells or their friends. They surely would have done so if they truly believed that she was the guilty party.

While the witch was not clear about identity, it was terribly clear about purpose, which was to destroy "Old Jack Bell." Just why the witch hated Bell so violently was never entirely clear. On the other hand, the witch adored John's wife, Lucy, or Luce, extolling her virtues while threatening and damning John.

The witch also took a new interest in Betsy. Joshua Gardner, a young man who lived nearby, announced that he intended to marry the girl, though, in fact, she was too young to marry. Still the witch didn't care for the idea at all. First, it pleaded with Betsy not to marry him; and when that didn't work, it began to torment her with pinches, slaps, and by giving her fainting fits. When a friend of Gardner's visited, the witch kept screaming at him and threatening him. Betsy never did marry Joshua Gardner.

The witch did not confine its interests to the Bell family alone. It took to gossiping about everyone in the area very loudly. No one was safe from the witch's malicious tongue. The pious James Johnson was referred to as "Old Sugar Mouth."

Yet the witch did not profess to be godless either. On a couple of occasions it was reported to have repeated the minister's sermon word for word after church.

The Bell Witch continued its activities for three years, and the strain began to tell on the family, particularly on John Bell. His health declined. He visited a doctor who gave him a variety of medicines, but none of them seemed to help. On the morning of December 19, 1820, Bell lapsed into a coma. One of his sons rushed to the cabinet where the medicines were kept, but instead of the usual bottles he found "a smoky looking vial, which was about one-third full of dark colored liquid." The doctor was sent for, but the witch announced that it was too late: "It's useless for you to try to revive Old Jack. I've got him this time. He'll never get up from that bed again!" When asked about the bottle with the strange-looking liquid, the witch said, "I put it there and gave Old Jack a big dose out of it last night while he was fast asleep, which fixed him."

The liquid in the bottle was tested on a cat, and the cat died instantly. John Bell lingered a bit longer. He died the following day. The witch was exultant. Even during the funeral the air was filled with loud and derisive shouts and songs.

After the death of John Bell, the witch gradually lost interest in the family. One night several months after Bell's death, the living room of the Bell house was suddenly filled with smoke. From the midst of the cloud the witch shouted, "I am going and will be gone for seven years. Good-bye to all!"

Seven years later, the witch did return briefly. By that time Betsy was gone; she had married a former schoolmaster turned politician. He was much older than she was, and much richer. John Bell, junior, had also married and moved away. But John Bell's widow and three sons remained in the house. For about two weeks they were plagued with strange noises and something that pulled off the bedclothes, but there were no voices. A married son, however, said he heard a voice announcing the witch would come again in one hundred and seven years. The prophesied year was 1934, but none of John Bell's living descendants reported any strange incidents that year.

By any standard, the story of the Bell Witch is an absolutely incredible one. So incredible that we are

forced to inquire about the quality of the evidence—
in short, how do we know these things really
happened?

Some twenty-six years after the Bell Witch first
made its appearance, Richard Williams Bell (usually
called Williams) set down his recollections in a book
called *Our Family Trouble*. The book was never published, and apparently was never intended for
publication.

Then, in 1891, Williams' son Allen turned the
manuscript over to a writer by the name of M. V.
Ingram, who rewrote it. It was then published with
one of those long titles that told the potential reader,
in some detail, what the book was going to be about:
*An Authenticated History of the Famous Bell Witch.
The Wonder of the 19th Century, and Unexplained
Phenomenon of the Christian Era. The Mysterious
Talking Goblin that Terrorized the West End of Rob-
ertson County, Tennessee, Tormenting John Bell to his
Death. The Story of Betsy Bell, Her Lover and the
Haunting Sphynx, Clarksville, Tenn.*

It was the sort of story that one might find today
in the tabloids on sale at supermarket checkout
counters. Back in 1891 such publications were called
"penny dreadfuls." Ingram was well versed in the
sensational style of writing. An example of Ingram's
style can be found in a letter, supposedly from a Colonel Thomas L. Yancy, describing a visit of General

General Andrew Jackson, who was said to have witnessed the disruptive phenomena created by the Bell Witch.

(later president) Andrew Jackson to the Bell house. Among those in Jackson's party was a professional "witch layer," who said that he would shoot the witch if it appeared. Jackson and his group gathered about, waiting for the witch.

"The General did not have long to wait. Presently perfect quiet reigned, and then was heard a noise like dainty footsteps prancing over the floor, and quickly following, the same metallic voice heard in the bushes rang out from one corner of the room, exclaiming 'All right, General, I am on hand ready for business.' And then addressing the witch layer, 'Now, Mr. Smarty, here I am, shoot.' The seer stroked his nose with the cat's tail, leveled his pistol, and pulled the trigger, but it failed to fire. 'Try again,' exclaimed the witch, which he did with the same result. 'Now it's my turn; look out you old coward, hypocrite, fraud. I'll teach you a lesson.' The next thing a sound was heard like that of boxing with the open hand, whack, whack, and the oracle tumbled over like lightning had struck him, but he quickly recovered his feet and went capering around the room like a frightened steer, running over everyone in his way yelling. 'Oh my nose, my nose, the devil has got me by the nose.' Suddenly, as if by its own accord, the door flew open and the witch layer dashed out, and made a bee line for the lane at full speed, yelling every jump. Every body rushed out under the excitement, expecting the man would be killed, but as far as they could hear up the lane, he was still running and yelling, 'Oh Lordy.' Jackson, they say, dropped down on the ground and rolled over and over laughing. 'By the eternal, boys, I never saw so much fun in all my life. This beats fighting the British.' Presently the witch was on hand and joined in the laugh. 'Lord Jesus,' it exclaimed, 'How the old devil did run and beg; I'll bet he won't come here again with his old horse pistol to shoot me. I guess that's fun enough for to-night, General, and you can go to bed now. I will come to-morrow night and show you another rascal in this crowd.' Old Hickory was anxious to stay a week, but his party had enough of that thing. No one knew whose turn would come next, and no inducement could keep them."

There is absolutely no confirming evidence that such a scene ever took place or that Andrew Jackson had the slightest interest in or knowledge of the Bell Witch.

The other sources of information are a small pamphlet written in 1930 by Harriet Parks Miller, who said she interviewed many people who had visited the Bell home during the "troubles." Four years later Charles Bailey Bell, M.D., great-grandson of the unfortunate John Bell wrote a longer and more influential pamphlet, *A Mysterious Spirit, The Bell Witch of Tennessee*. Dr. Bell said that he got much of his information from Betsy Bell herself. She lived to the age of eighty-three, and was apparently very fond of re-lating Bell Witch tales. Both books, by the way, are still sold in Clarksville, Tennessee, near the site of the Bell home. The story is still told to tourists, though how deeply it is believed, it is difficult to say.

One need not be a hardened skeptic to be skeptical of the evidence. Even if one were to assume that the authors were not simply making things up—and in Ingram's case, at least, that is a dubious assumption —they are talking about incidents that happened a long, long time before they set any words on paper. Williams, who is the sole firsthand witness whose tes-timony we possess, was only six years old when the Bell Witch manifestations began. How much could he accurately remember, and how much of what he did remember was rewritten by Ingram? We cannot answer such questions.

Still, something probably happened to get the Bell Witch legend started in the first place. To most leg-ends there is at least a kernel of truth around which a great deal of exaggeration may accumulate. I suspect that the kernel of truth in this case is a poltergeist. Except for the witch's speech, most of the other phe-nomena attributed to it are typical of a poltergeist.

Another typical feature is that the excitement seemed to center around a young person, in this case twelve-year-old Betsy Bell. During the period of the witch visitations Betsy was often thrown into a very strange state. She was "subjected to fainting spells followed by prostration, characterized by shortness of breath and smothering sensations, panting as it were for life, and became entirely exhausted and lifeless, losing her breath for nearly a minute between gasps, and rendered unconscious. These spells lasted from thirty to forty minutes, and passed off as suddenly, leaving her perfectly restored after a few minutes, in which she recovered from the exhaustion. There is no positive evidence that these spells were produced by the witch. However, that was the conclusion from the fact that no other cause was apparent. She is a very stout girl and, with this exception, the personification of robust health, and was never subject to hysteria or anything of the kind. Moreover, the spells came on at regular hours in the evening, just at the time the witch usually appeared; and immediately after the spells passed off, the mysterious voice commenced talking but never uttered a word during the time of prostration."

Some of the Bells' neighbors suspected that Betsy was responsible for all the strange goings-on. They tried to test her in a variety of ways. For example, at one point a doctor clamped his hand over Betsy's mouth while the voice of the witch was heard, to make sure that Betsy was not "throwing her voice." According to the accounts, Betsy passed all the tests.

But as I've already pointed out, the accounts were not necessarily reliable.

Finally, did Betsy Bell actually contrive to kill her own father? She was never prosecuted for it, much less convicted. Perhaps John Bell simply died from natural causes during the period, and local gossip immediately assumed that the famous witch was responsible. It is also possible that Betsy did have something to do with her father's death.

In this case, as in so many others, we don't know what happened, and we never will. The Bell Witch must remain a tantalizing and mysterious bit of American folklore.

SEVEN

Christmas Ghosts

WHAT IS THE BEST TIME OF YEAR FOR reading and telling ghost stories?

I can almost hear you all shouting—"Halloween!" And you would be right, today. But a century or so ago Halloween was barely noticed. Yet people did read and tell ghost stories, and they did so on what seems to us to be a most unlikely holiday—Christmas.

What is the most famous ghost story ever written?

It is Charles Dickens' *A Christmas Carol*. Think about it for a minute. The whole thing starts with Marley's ghost, and there are the various spirits of Christmas. In fact, Dickens himself subtitled his tale "A Ghost Story of Christmas."

Many of the best ghost stories of the late nineteenth and early twentieth centuries appeared in the big, glossy Christmas annuals put out by British and American publishers. These stories were eagerly read to and by children and adults alike over the long nights of the Christmas holidays, when the house was lit only by gaslights or oil lamps, and there was, of course, no television.

But why this connection between the joyful religious holiday of Christmas and the gloomy and often irreligious ghost story? The tradition seems limited to the British, and to a lesser extent, to Americans who were influenced by English traditions and fashions. I had speculated that the tradition might go back to pre-Christian times, and to some pagan celebration of the winter solstice. Many Christmas traditions, like the lighted Christmas tree and mistletoe, do go back that far.

The date of Christmas itself seems to have been fixed in late December in order to be associated with, and ultimately replace, a pagan winter celebration. Certainly the date of Christ's birth is not given in the Bible, and Christmas was not even celebrated until sometime in the fourth century. Even then there was a great deal of theological wrangling over the proper date, and Christmas is still celebrated on different dates in different parts of the Christian world.

So I had assumed that the ghost stories were part

of an old pagan tradition. The costumes and ghostly tales associated with Halloween came from pagan times. Halloween itself is the evening before the important religious holiday of All Saints' Day, but the time was also one of a pagan festival of autumn.

The same sort of combination of traditions could account for the Christmas ghost story. That's what I assumed anyway, but I wasn't sure. I checked references on medieval English Christmas traditions, but could find no mention of the telling of ghost stories. The American author Washington Irving had apparently heard something of the tradition when he lived in England in the early 1800s, but was unable to find anyone who actually told ghost stories at Christmas. I talked to lots of people, from English historians to spirit mediums. None of them had the faintest notion where the tradition came from, though they all were aware of it.

At least part of the mystery was cleared up for me by E. F. Bleiler, an authority on supernatural fiction, particularly of the Victorian era.

Bleiler believes that the tradition of the Christmas ghost story can be traced, in large measure, to Charles Dickens and the enormous popular success of *A Christmas Carol*. "Dickens' *Christmas Carol* (1843), in all probability, had much to do with linking Christmas with ghosts, but it is not clear whether it reinflated an older, weak tradition or created a new configuration."

Marley's ghost from Charles Dickens' A Christmas Carol.
*This story was so popular that it may have started the
tradition of reading ghost stories at Christmastime.*

Before *A Christmas Carol*, the Christmas book "was a small, daintily bound, pretentious collection of sugary verse and mushy engravings, a gift for a maiden aunt or a platonic sweetheart." After *A Christmas Carol*, ghost stories were included regularly, along with games, plays, songs—a whole collection of things which were to entertain children during the holidays.

That brings up another interesting point for the collector and teller of ghost stories: Ghost stories were children's entertainment not only at Christmastime, but throughout the year. Today parents and educators worry a great deal about the effects of monster movies or violent television shows on delicate young minds. But back in the Victorian era, when children were supposed to be fragile little creatures with flowing curls, parents and nursemaids used to give children the creeps, or just plain scare the daylights out of them, by telling them ghastly ghost stories at bedtime. Nurseries resounded with stories of ghostly gray ladies with slit throats, or of the ghosts of children who had been beaten or starved to death coming back to haunt their wicked stepmothers. Perhaps Victorian children had stronger nerves than today's television generation. Or perhaps children of all eras just like being scared by ghost stories sometimes.

Where did these stories come from? Bleiler believes that a good percentage of them came directly out of psychical research. Many of the popular Victorian ghost stories were merely dramatized or fictionalized versions of the sort of accounts that were being collected by the Society for Psychical Research. A lot of people believed in ghosts, and thought they had seen them. That is why ghost stories were so popular.

The S.P.R. wasn't particularly happy about being associated with Christmas ghosts. In 1884 an S.P.R. publication complained:

"In the magazine ghost stories, which appear in such numbers every Christmas, the ghost is a fearsome being, dressed in a sweeping sheet or shroud, carrying a lighted candle, and squeaking dreadful words from fleshless lips. It enters at the stroke of midnight, through the sliding panel, just by the blood stain on the floor, which no effort could ever remove. Or it may be only a clinking of chains, a tread as of armed men, heard whilst the candles burn blue, and the dogs howl. These are the ghosts of fiction, and we do not deny that now and then we receive, apparently on good authority, accounts of apparitions which are stated to exhibit some features of a sensational type. Such cases, however, are very rare, and must for the present be dismissed as exceptional."

But as Bleiler points out, the S.P.R.'s opinion in this respect was wrong. The ghosts of fiction were modeled far more closely on the factual accounts collected by psychical researchers than the S.P.R. knew or cared to admit.

Besides, the best of the Christmas ghost stories were not supposed to be fiction. They were presented to the reader as fact. They were usually second- or third-hand—someone retelling what he had heard from Lord Such-and-Such about the ghost that had chased his great-uncle into the moat—that sort of thing. That is not the sort of evidence that would satisfy the S.P.R., but it satisfied a lot of tellers of "true" ghost stories.

Some people became quite well known for their personal collections of ghost stories. Among them was Lord Halifax. Over half a century ago, Lord Halifax's son had his father's private ghost story collection published for the enjoyment of the general public. It is still popular today. In introducing the collection he wrote:

> "As long as I can remember, my father's *Ghost Book* was one of the most distinctive associations of Hickleton [the family home]. He kept it always with great care himself, from time to time making additions to it in his own handwriting, and bringing it out on special occasions, such as Christmas, to read some of the particular favourites aloud before we all went to bed. Many is the time that after such an evening we children would hurry upstairs, feeling that the distance

between the library and our nurseries, dimly lit by oil lamps and full of shadows, was a danger area where we would not willingly go alone, and where it was unsafe to dawdle.

"Such treatment of young nerves, in those days, would not have been everybody's prescription; and I well recollect my mother protesting—though almost invariably to no effect—against 'the children being frightened too much.' My father, however, used to justify the method as calculated to stimulate the imagination, and the victims themselves, fascinated and spellbound by a sense of delicious terror, never failed to ask for more."

Here then are some typical Christmas ghost stories featuring children, which were collected by Lord Halifax and others.

THIS ONE, which appeared in *Lord Halifax's Ghost Book*, was sent to him by Lady Margaret Shelley, who kept her own ghost book. It was supposed to have taken place during the mid-nineteenth century.

A woman and her two daughters were staying at a house at Sutten Verney, in the north of England. As the house was very full, the two girls shared a room. The older girl had a bed; the younger one slept in a cot nearby.

In the middle of the night, the older girl woke up with the distinct feeling of a child's head resting on her shoulder. She thought it was her sister who had climbed into bed with her. But when she lit a candle, she saw her sister sound asleep in the cot. She blew out the candle and began to drop off to sleep when she had exactly the same feeling. This time she stretched out her hand to where the child's head should have been, but nothing was there. After that she was unable to get back to sleep.

The girl retold this story many times, and one time a person she told it to added a postscript. "I know you are talking of Sutten Verney. We bought the place and that room became such a difficulty that at last we pulled down the wing in which it was situated. When the men broke up the floor, they discovered a cavity in which were the skeletons of five children."

ANOTHER SUPPOSEDLY TRUE event recorded in *Lord Halifax's Ghost Book* took place in 1835. The family involved was the Carnsens, who lived in the county of Cornwall. Lord Halifax apparently got the story from one of the young women who had actually been present.

John Carnsen, aged eleven, had been taken seriously ill. For some weeks no one was sure whether he was going to live or die. Then quite suddenly he began to feel better. Though the doctors cautioned that no real improvement had taken place, his brothers and sisters were much cheered by this turn of events. They began to think that they had been worrying unnecessarily.

One evening at the end of March, a "piercing shriek rang through the house. It was as if uttered by someone standing on the landing just outside the open door [of John's bedroom].

> "There was a silence, and then a second shriek like the first; another silence, and then yet a third shriek, even louder and more prolonged than the others, and ending in a rattling, gurgling sound, as though someone were dying."

Naturally everyone was absolutely terrified, and they began charging around trying to find out where the sound had come from and who had made it. But no one seemed to know. One of the servants became hysterical and said that the sound was "no human voice" and that now there was "no hope for Master John."

It was then that the people in the house suddenly remembered the sick boy. They rushed upstairs, fearing that the horrible noise would have frightened him, or that he might have had some sort of fit and cried out himself. In the room were the boy, his mother, and an aunt. They were all sitting quietly. None of them had heard anything and they all said that they had not been asleep. Yet the noise had undoubtedly come from a spot very close to the boy's room, and everyone outside of the room heard it clearly.

The family was at a loss to explain what had caused the awful noise or what it meant. But they began to despair for the boy's life, though his health still appeared to be improving. Then he took a sudden turn for the worse, and died three weeks to the day on which the three shrieks had been heard.

FINALLY, HERE IS A mournful little tale that has been used by generations of parents to frighten generations of reluctant students. It concerns William Hoby, the son of Sir Thomas Hoby, who lived in the time of King Henry VIII.

The boy's parents were both brilliant and energetic people, though his mother had always been considered rather odd. Aside from being a scholar in several languages, Lady Hoby had also been described as "a pest of outstanding quality." Poor William inherited none of his family's intellectual gifts. Not only was he a slow learner, he was sloppy as well. During his lessons he became so nervous that he always made ink blots in his copybook. Lady Hoby was severely disappointed in her son, and the blotted copybooks never failed to enrage her. William was frequently beaten because of his poor work. One day Lady Hoby became so enraged that she completely lost control of herself and beat the boy to death.

The place where William died is called Bisham Abbey. It was said to be haunted not only by poor little William's ghost, but by the ghost of Lady Hoby. This ghost was seen washing her hands in a basin which floated before her. According to one account, the ghost was seen "in negative" that is, with a black face and hands and wearing a white dress.

In the nineteenth century, renovations were made at Bisham Abbey. Behind one of the walls was found a number of badly blotted copybooks. According to tradition, these were the very books which drove Lady Hoby into her murderous fury.

After World War II, the abbey was taken over by a sports organization and converted into a gymnasium and hostel for students. The ghosts have not been reported since that time.

EIGHT

Some American Ghosts

BY NOW YOU MAY HAVE GOTTEN THE
feeling that ghosts are only reported in crumbling
English castles or stately manor houses. Or that all
ghost stories concern things that happened a long time
ago.

Not at all. Ghosts are still being reported today,
sometimes in places that might be very like the home
in which you live. Here are some examples of encounters with ghostly children in modern America.

THE FEBRUARY, 1976, issue of *Fate* magazine,
probably America's leading publication on strange
and sometimes ghostly events, contains a tale of an

encounter with a quite modern child ghost. The account was written by Marilis Hornidge. She described how she was helping a friend move into a house in Larchmont, New York, a suburb of New York City. The house was not very old or very creepy looking. It was the last place you would think of finding a ghost, but Miss Hornidge says she found one, or rather one found her.

After a day of unpacking, Miss Hornidge and her friend were resting in front of the fire when they heard a strange rhythmic noise coming from one of the upstairs rooms.

The sound was not very ominous, not like the clanking of chains or loud moaning that is attributed to the traditional ghost. It sounded more like a bouncing ball. But still it made them feel uncomfortable, and they decided to go upstairs to investigate. The noise sounded as if it were coming from a small suite of rooms on the third floor. As they approached the rooms, Miss Hornidge noted something strange. All the other bedrooms in the house had latches on the inside and outside, high enough so a child could not reach them.

The suite was filled with half-unpacked boxes but nothing else they could see. As Miss Hornidge turned to leave, she felt a tug at her skirt. Thinking she had caught the skirt on a nail, she reached down, and suddenly her hand was grasped by what felt like a tiny ice-cold hand. Somehow its icy hold "communicated a feeling of panic and painful loneliness. I wanted to look down—but I *couldn't*."

She walked straight out of the room and said nothing to her friend. As she left the room the icy hand loosened its grasp and faded away, but Miss Hornidge's hand remained cold all night.

After that the house was troubled by occasional strange noises, but only when Miss Hornidge was a guest. It was much later, after her friend had moved from the house, that Miss Hornidge learned that one of the previous owners had a retarded daughter who had died young. Most of the unfortunate child's life had been spent locked in the suite on the third floor. Her favorite toy was a ball, which she bounced endlessly against the wall.

WHEN THE PUBLICATION *USA Weekend* appealed to its readers for stories of ghostly encounters to publish in a Halloween issue, they were overwhelmed by hundreds of responses. They were able to use only a tiny fraction of these accounts in their regular issue. But a collection of some of the best were published in 1992 in a book called *I Never Believed in Ghosts Until . . .* The editors changed the names in the stories to protect the privacy of the individuals, but say that otherwise the stories are as they were submitted.

One by a woman who is called Carla S. Mazurik tells of a somewhat happier encounter with a lonely child ghost. Mrs. Mazurik and her family moved into an old farmhouse that was built in 1878. Shortly after moving in she became aware of a "presence." "As time went on, we would often catch a glimpse of a white wisp peeking around the barn and disappearing; sometimes it would look around from the side of the house. Since it stood as tall as the bottom of the electric meter on the house, we assumed it to be a child."

Later she heard that a little girl who had lived in a nearby house many years ago had knocked over a kerosene lamp and burned to death. She could never discover if this was the identity of the ghost, but it seemed likely.

One of the oddest manifestations of this particular ghost was that it appeared to play music, but the music was never loud enough to be identified.

One Christmas the ghost broke a glass on the kitchen floor. It was the only time it had ever become violent. Mrs. Mazurik thought that the ghost was up-set about not getting a Christmas present. "I bought a small teddy bear for her. For a period of time after that, the bear was frequently moved, as if it had been played with. Since then, I have bought her a gift every Christmas, but she does not seem to touch them."

Over the years the visits from the ghost have become less frequent. Mrs. Mazurik wondered if the ghost had not been drawn to the house at the time her children were small, but had become less interested as the children grew up.

ANOTHER *USA Weekend* account was attributed to Tracy M. Sabo. In this case the ghost was a very familiar one, her brother Christian. He had been struck by lightning and killed on July 5, 1961. He was nine and one-half at the time. Tracy was only four, and had idolized her "big brother."

The ghost, however, did not appear for nearly ten years, and by that time the family had moved to New Jersey. One afternoon Tracy thought she saw her brother Evan run out of the kitchen and upstairs. Evan had been born just three weeks after Christian had been killed.

Tracy ran after the figure, calling for him to stop. But he didn't; he ran upstairs and simply disappeared. She searched every room in the house but couldn't find him. Later Evan came in and claimed he hadn't been home all day.

"The little boy I chased had blond hair and was wearing beige shorts and a red, white, and blue striped shirt. Christian, who had short blond hair, was wearing beige shorts and a striped shirt when he was killed."

The spirit of Christian continued to make its presence known, even after Tracy left the family home and moved into her own apartment. Now the manifestations were primarily small handprints on the wall. "The prints looked as if they were made by someone who had first touched a newspaper—they were black and strong and visible to anyone. Sometimes you could see just a few fingers; other times the whole hand from thumb to pinky was there. Once the whole handprint appeared over my bed, right above my head."

Tracy compared the prints to her own hand, but found they were much smaller. She could not have made them herself by accident.

Far from finding this ghostly manifestation frightening, Tracy has found the small handprints comforting and reassuring. They have appeared at times when her own life has been troubled and she has taken them as a sign that her "big brother" is still watching out for her.

ANOTHER TALE OF ghostly children was collected by the writer Susy Smith for her book *Prominent American Ghosts*. This one concerns a genuinely historic house, the old Robert E. Lee mansion in Alexandria, Virginia. But the haunting itself is modern.

In 1962, the house was purchased by investment broker Henry Koch and his family. Though they knew the history of the house well enough, they had never heard that it had a reputation for being haunted. But soon after they moved in, they were confronted by a series of puzzling manifestations. The most persistent of these was the sound of running footsteps and childish laughter.

Now the patter of little feet around the house is supposed to be one of the most cheerful of domestic sounds. However, when no children can be found who made these sounds, they can become rather unnerving. But the Koch family soon got used to them. And the ghost, if that's what it was, turned out to be exceptionally well behaved. It did not run about giggling in the middle of the night, waking up the residents. It confined its activities to the daylight hours.

Mrs. Koch is quoted as saying, "It would walk along with us, giggling. It sounded as if it were coming from a child about four years old; the laughter was at about the level of our knees."

For a while the sounds were quite frequent, but after about six months they began to fade away. "It was so cheery," said Mrs. Koch, "that we were really disappointed when we stopped hearing it so often."

Were these sounds caused by the spirit of a Lee who had died young in that house? A check of the Lee family history shows that Robert E. Lee did have a child who was killed at about the age of four in a fall down a flight of steps. But that happened after the Lee family left the house in Alexandria and had moved back to the much larger and more elegant family home about fifty miles away.

The Lee family had occupied the Alexandria house during an unhappy period. Robert E. Lee's father, Light-Horse Harry Lee, had lost a great deal of money in financial speculations, had been jailed twice, and then ran off to the island of Barbados. His wife moved out of the Lee mansion at Stratford, Virginia, to the house in Alexandria, which was lent to them by a friend. Robert E. Lee was about three at that time.

Light-Horse Harry died before he was able to return to his family. The Lees stayed in the Alexandria house until Robert entered West Point at the age of eighteen. Then they moved back to Stratford.

Of course, the Alexandria house is quite an old one. Parts of it date back to 1770. It is more than possible that a young child died in the house at some point during its long history. The Lees lived there only a short time. But, because they were the house's most famous residents, the house is called the Lee house, and the ghost is usually attributed to the Lees.

According to Susy Smith, who said she was "psychically sensitive," the house gave her a kind of odd feeling. "As I walked into the back part of the downstairs hall under the landing, I got a prickly sensation along my spine. It was not a scary feeling—actually it was more like the delicious chills you get when someone kisses your ear or the back of your neck."

But unquestionably the strangest manifestation

*General Robert E. Lee, whose historic mansion in
Alexandria, Virginia, was said to be haunted
by the ghost of a child.*

ever encountered in the house, whether caused by ghosts or not, was the phantom snowflakes. One Sunday afternoon some neighbors came over to visit. Then, without any warning, one of the visitors, the wife of a retired admiral, was surrounded by what appeared to be fat white snowflakes. The flakes seemed to start about a foot above the woman's head. The windows and ceiling were checked for some sort of leak, but nothing was found. The flakes stopped, then started again as she began to leave. No one seems to have a plausible explanation for the occurrence.

LOUISA E. RHINE was the wife of J. B. Rhine, who had been the leading figure in American parapsychology for many years. But she was also an investigator in her own right. For most of their long careers, the Rhines had been involved with laboratory tests for extrasensory perception, or ESP. But they did not neglect the more traditional side of psychical research, collecting accounts of strange occurrences —what we sometimes call ghost stories. Here is one that she recounted in her book, *PSI: What Is It?*

The story concerns an unnamed family that lived in an old mansion in southern California. Though the family had lived there many years, the house was old when they bought it, and its origins were unknown. In 1943, during World War II, the father was away in the army and the mother was in the hospital with appendicitis. The daughter, Mary, who was five years old, was being watched over by her grandmother.

One day Mary and her grandmother went down into the cellar, and Mary saw an Indian girl with long black hair, moccasins, and an old brown dress, standing in the corner staring at her. Mary was frightened and began to cry. She told her grandmother about the Indian girl. But the grandmother saw nothing, and accused Mary of telling lies. She also warned the girl not to tell her mother anything, so as not to worry her when she came home from the hospital.

As the years passed, Mary gradually convinced herself that the incident had never really happened, that she had made the whole thing up, just as her grandmother had said. Later, Mary moved away, married, and had her own family. Then one Christmas she took her two little girls, aged five and eight, back to the house in California for a visit.

The two girls began exploring the old house, and went into the cellar. A few minutes later they ran upstairs screaming. The younger one had seen the Indian girl staring at her. She became so frightened that she had frightened her sister, who had seen nothing.

Mrs. Rhine commented: "The story could be called a case of haunting; and if two five-year-olds saw the figure, even though a generation apart, it would seem that it must reflect some kind of reality. Of course, it was not actually an Indian girl, because neither of the other persons present on either occasion saw her. Both children experienced an hallucination.

"The question is: Why?"

Mrs. Rhine offers three possible explanations which would be acceptable to parapsychologists. The first is that there had been an Indian girl associated with the cellar sometime in the past, and that the two girls had, in some unknown way, been given a glimpse of the past.

Second, that there had been no Indian girl associated with the cellar, and that the first experience was indeed imaginary. "The second little girl's experience, then, could have been based on it, possibly by ESP of the telepathic kind." Mrs. Rhine does not mention the possibility that the first experience might have been imaginary, and that Mary had mentioned it to her younger child. Perhaps she did not recall having done so. This might in turn have stimulated the second child's imagination to "see" what her mother had "seen." Nothing extrasensory need have been involved at all.

Mrs. Rhine's third possibility is a genuine ghost. "If the Indian girl had actually existed and her spirit caused the two sensitive children to have hallucinatory impressions of her, it would have been a survival case."

AND FINALLY there is the haunting that survived the house.

Near the town of Sodus, in upstate New York, about halfway between Rochester and Oswego, people talk about the spot where, when a thunderstorm threatens, you can hear the crying and whimpering of a baby.

Years ago, a widow and her one-year-old daughter had lived in a house at that spot. The sudden death of her husband had affected the woman's mind.

One night, during a severe thunderstorm, the poor woman appears to have cracked. No one is sure exactly what happened, but when the neighbors came to the house the following morning they found the woman cowering on the floor, unable to speak. The baby was dead in its crib. It appeared as if the woman, in a moment of intense rage or frenzy, killed her child to keep it from crying. The mother died a few weeks later without ever uttering a word.

People who passed the now empty house said they could hear a baby crying inside whenever a thunderstorm was brewing. About a year after the tragedy, the house was struck by lightning and burned to a smoldering ruin. Still, the sound of the crying baby was heard during storms.

The neighbors could stand it no longer. They got together and tore down the chimney and fireplace, the only part of the house left standing. The stones were scattered throughout the countryside. All visible traces of the house were covered up.

Still, if you stand in the clearing where the house once was, and the skies turn black with the approach of a storm, you can hear the faint cry of a child.

BIBLIOGRAPHY

Bardens, Dennis. *Ghosts and Hauntings*. London: Zeus Press, 1965

Bell, Charles Bailey and Harriet Parks Miller. *The Bell Witch of Tennessee*. Nashville, Tennessee: Charles Elder. Facsimile Reproduction, 1972

Bleiler, E. F., ed. *The Collected Ghost Stories of Mrs. J. H. Riddell*. New York: Dover Publications, 1977

Braddock, Joseph. *Haunted Houses*. London: Batsford, 1956

Canning, John, ed. *50 Great Ghost Stories*. New York: Bell, 1971

Carrington, Hereward and Nandor Fodor. *Haunted People*. New York: Signet, 1968

Cohen, Daniel. *In Search of Ghosts*. New York: Dodd, Mead, 1972

Curran, Ronald, ed. *Witches, Wraiths & Warlocks*. New York: Fawcett World Library, 1971

Dingwall, Eric J. and Trevor H. Hall. *Four Modern Ghosts*. London: Duckworth, 1958

Hornidge, Marilis. "Lonely Little Ghost in the 3rd Floor Suite." *Fate*, February 1976, pp. 65–66

Lindley, Charles, Viscount Halifax. *Lord Halifax's Ghost Book*. London: Geoffrey Bles, 1936

Podmore, Frank. *Mediums of the 19th Century*. New Hyde Park, N.Y.: University Books, 1963

Rhine, Louisa E. *PSI: What Is It?* New York: Harper & Row, 1975

Sidgwick, Eleanor M., ed. *Phantasms of the Living*. New Hyde Park, N.Y.: University Books, 1962

Smith, Susy. *Prominent American Ghosts*. New York: World, 1967

Somerlott, Robert. *Here Mr. Splitfoot*. New York: Viking Press, 1971

Thomas, Keith. *Religion and the Decline of Magic*. New York: Charles Scribner's Sons, 1971

Underwood, Peter. *A Gazetteer of British Ghosts*. New York: Walker & Co., 1971

Editors of *USA Weekend. I Never Believed in Ghosts Until* . . . Chicago: Contemporary Books, 1992

INDEX

Andrews, Miles Peter, 12
Apparitions. *See* Children as
    apparitions

Bardens, Dennis, 59
Batts, Kate, 67–68
Bell, Charles Bailey, 62, 74
Bell, Elizabeth (Betsy), 65, 67,
    68–69, 74–75, 76–77
Bell, John, 62, 64–65, 68, 70, 74
Bell, Lucy, 68
Bell, Richard Williams, 64, 71
Bell Witch, The, 63–77
Bisham Abbey, 89
Bleiler, E. F., 80, 82, 83
Borley Rectory, 45, 47, 51
Bowyer-Bower, Captain Eldred,
    30–32
Bridge, Lieutenant G. E. W., 33
Bulwer-Lytton, Edward (Baron
    Lytton of Knebworth), 10–
    11

Carnsen, John, 86–88
Castlereagh, Viscount (Captain
    Robert Stewart), 5–10
Chater, Mrs. Cecily, 31
Children
  and ghosts, 1–3
  as apparitions, 4, 5, 6, 10, 12,
    14, 22, 32, 35, 36–43, 86,
    91–92, 93

as poltergeists, 52–61, 75–76
effect of ghost stories on, 82,
    84–85
supernatural events seen by,
    29, 33–34, 86, 100–101
Christmas Carol, A (Dickens),
    78, 80, 82
Christmas ghosts, 2, 78–89
Corby Castle, 13–15
Court records, ghost stories
    based on, 18

Dickens, Charles, 16, 78, 80, 81
Dingwall, Eric, 47, 49–51
Du Cane sisters, 33, 34

England
  Christmas ghost stories in,
    78–79, 80, 82, 84–89
  ghost story popularity in, 90
Epworth Parsonage, 55–59, 60
ESP (extrasensory perception),
    99, 101

Fate magazine, 90
Fifty Years of Psychical Research
    (Price), 43

Gardner, Joshua, 68–69
Ghosts
  avenging, 17–25
  crimes deterred by, 18

harmlessness of, 22, 53
portents by, 4, 9, 12, 29–30, 32, 35, 88
protective, 18
Ghosts and Hauntings (Bardens), 59
Goldney, Mrs. K.M., 44–45, 48, 51

Halifax, Lord, 84–85
Hall, Trevor, 49–50, 51
Harris, George, 19–24
Hoby, Sir Thomas and Lady, 88–89
Hoby, William, 88–89
Hornidge, Marilis, 91–92
Howard family, 14–15

I Never Believed in Ghosts Until . . . , 92
Indian girl ghost, 100–101
Ingram, M.V., 71, 73–74

Jackson, Andrew, 72, 73–74
Johnson, James, 65, 69
Jones, Ellen, 32–33

Koch, Henry and family, 95–96

Lee, Light-Horse Harry, 97
Lee, Robert E., 95, 96, 98
Lord Halifax's Ghost Book, 84, 85, 86

Materialization. *See* Rosalie case
Mazurik, Carla S., 93–94
Mediums, spirit. *See* Séances. *See also* Rosalie case
Miller, Harriet Parks, 74–75
Morris, Richard, 19–22, 24–25

Myers, Frederic, 26
Mysterious Spirit, The Bell Witch of Tennessee, A (Bell), 74

National Laboratory of Psychical Research, 51

"Old Jeffrey," 58–59
Our Family Trouble (Bell), 71

Parapsychological research, 27–28, 99. *See also* Society for Psychical Research
Penny dreadfuls, 18, 71
Podmore, Frank, 54–55, 59, 60
Poltergeists, 52–61, 63, 75
harmful, 53
theories about, 53
Price, Harry, 36–47, 49, 50, 51
Prominent American Ghosts (Smith), 95
PSI: What Is It? (Rhine), 99
Psychical research, 27–28, 37, 44, 49
ghost stories based on, 82–83
theories in, 101–102
See also Society for Psychical Research

Radiant Boy legends, 2, 4–15
Rector of Greystoke, 14–15
Rhine, J. B., 99
Rhine, Louisa E., 99–101
Robertson County, Tennessee, 64, 67
Rosalie case, 36–51
house in, 39–40, 42, 49–50
Russell, Mrs. E. S., 29–30

Sabo, Tracy M., 94–95

Shelley, Lady Margaret, 85–86
Sidgwick, Eleanor M., 34
Smith, Susy, 95, 97, 99
Society for Psychical Research (S.P.R.), 2, 27–35, 83–84
Sodus, New York, 102
Spearman, Mrs., 30
S.P.R. See Society for Psychical Research
Supernatural events. See Children, supernatural events seen by

Tabori, Dr. Paul, 37
Tarwell, Richard, 19, 20–25

USA Weekend, 92, 94

Victorian ghost stories, 82–83

Ward, E. M., 11
Watson, Mrs., 31–32
Wesley, Emily, 60–61
Wesley, Hetty, 60, 61
Wesley, John, 55, 56, 57, 59, 60
Wesley, Mrs. (John's mother), 55–57, 58
Wesley, Reverend (John's father), 57–58
Wright, Annie, 34–35

Yancey, Colonel Thomas L., 71–74
Yellow Boy, the, 11